D1560751

THIS LAND CALLED AMERICA: **VERMONT**

CREATIVE EDUCATION

Published by Creative Education
P.O. Box 227, Mankato, Minnesota 56002
Creative Education is an imprint of The Creative Company
www.thecreativecompany.us

Design by Blue Design (www.bluedes.com)
Art direction by Rita Marshall
Book production by The Design Lab
Printed in the United States of America

Photographs by 123RF (Tom Oliveira), Alamy (David R. Frazier Photolibrary,
Inc., Mark Goodreau, The London Art Archive, North Wind Picture Archives),
The Bridgeman Art Library (Jean Antoine Gudin), Corbis (Bettmann, James
P. Blair, Clive Druett/Papilio, Kevin Fleming, Mark Gamba, Bob Krist, H.
Armstrong Roberts, Bob Sacha, Phil Schermeister, Dale C. Spartas, Michael S.
Yamashita), Dreamstime (Gkuchera), Getty Images (Craig Line, Steve Liss//
Time & Life Pictures, Clifford G. Scofield)

Library of Congress Cataloging-in-Publication Data
Gilbert, Sara.
Vermont / by Sara Gilbert.
p. cm. — (This land called America)
Includes bibliographical references and index.
ISBN 978-1-58341-798-0
1. Vermont—Juvenile literature. I. Title. II. Series.
F49.3.G55 2009
974.3—dc22   2008009529

First Edition
9 8 7 6 5 4 3 2 1

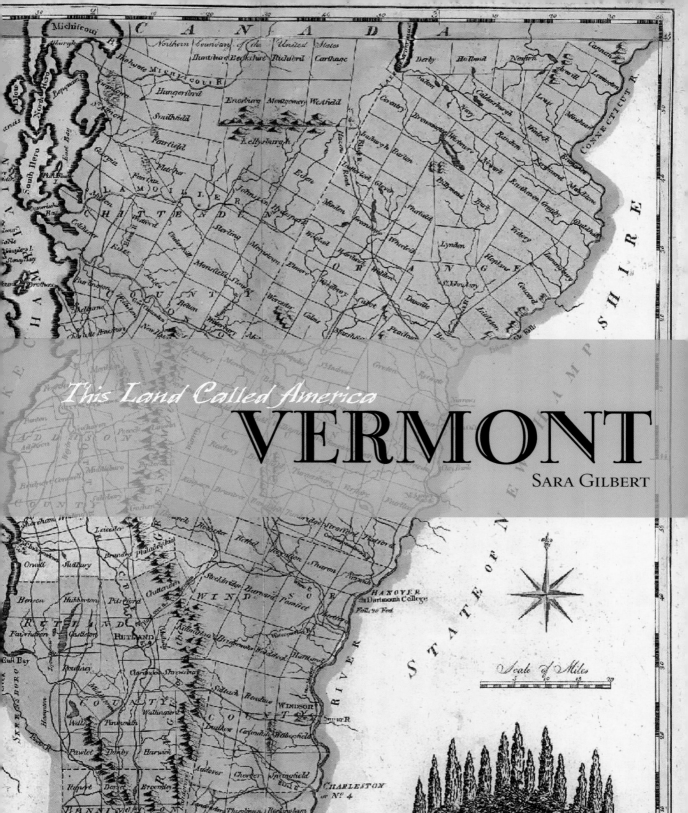

This Land Called America

VERMONT

Sara Gilbert

Vermont

SARA GILBERT

SPRING IN VERMONT SMELLS LIKE MAPLE
SYRUP. AS THE SNOW BEGINS TO MELT, THE
SAP IN THE BRANCHES OF THE STATE'S MANY
MAPLE TREES BEGINS TO RUN. THAT'S WHEN
LOCALS PUT ON THICK RUBBER BOOTS AND
MARCH INTO THE FOREST TO DRILL HOLES
IN THE TREES AND COLLECT MAPLE SYRUP.
AS THE STICKY SAP DRIPS INTO BUCKETS, A
SWEET SMELL SPREADS THROUGH THE AIR.
THE BUCKETS FILL QUICKLY. THEY HAVE TO
BE EMPTIED SEVERAL TIMES A DAY. IT IS HARD
WORK, BUT IT IS WORTH IT WHEN BREAKFAST
COMES. PANCAKES COVERED WITH PURE MAPLE
SYRUP TASTE EVEN BETTER IN VERMONT.

YEAR

1609　French explorer Samuel de Champlain claims the area that will become Vermont for France.

EVENT

Independent Beginnings

IN 1535, FRENCH EXPLORER JACQUES CARTIER WAS
THE FIRST EUROPEAN TO SEE WHAT IS NOW VERMONT.
ALMOST 70 YEARS LATER, ANOTHER FRENCH EXPLORER,
SAMUEL DE CHAMPLAIN, WAS SENT SOUTH FROM
QUEBEC, CANADA, TO INVESTIGATE MORE OF THE AREA.
HE FOUND SEVERAL TRIBES OF AMERICAN INDIANS,

including the Abenaki, the Mahican, and the Iroquois. The Indians lived off the land. They harvested maple syrup, hunted moose, deer, and caribou, and gathered plants and berries. They were afraid of Champlain's guns, so they fled when he and his men came to the area.

Champlain quickly claimed the land for France, a country that had already settled parts of Canada to the north. He named the enormous lake on its border for himself. The French built Fort Sainte Anne to protect the territory.

Then, in the early 1700s, other European settlers came to Vermont. The English, who had already claimed land in present-day Massachusetts, moved into the southeastern

Not long after Jacques Cartier discovered the St. Lawrence River to the north of Vermont (opposite), Samuel de Champlain also explored the area (above).

English settlers establish Fort Dummer, the first permanent settlement in Vermont.

corner of Vermont in 1724. They built Fort Dummer to protect their own cities farther south in the colonies of New York and Massachusetts. In 1761, the English also established the city of Bennington.

England and France battled for control of Vermont for many years. In 1763, England officially took control of Vermont. But by then, the people who had built homes in Vermont and struggled to survive during the long, harsh winters did not want to be under English rule. They wanted to be an independent state.

Led by Ethan Allen and his militia of ordinary people—called the Green Mountain Boys—the people of Vermont fought for independence. In 1777, the people voted to form their own republic, which they would call the free and independent State of Vermont. The name Vermont came from the French words *vert* (meaning "green") and *mont* (meaning "mount"). Vermont printed its own money. It operated its own postal service. It even had its own constitution, which gave every man the right to vote and made slavery illegal.

Ethan Allen and another famous Revolutionary figure, Benedict Arnold, led the attack on Fort Ticonderoga.

In the meantime, the 13 official American colonies were still fighting for independence from English rule in the Revolutionary War. In 1783, the colonies won the war and formed the United States. Even though Vermont was not one of the

YEAR

1775 Vermonter Ethan Allen and his Green Mountain Boys capture the English Fort Ticonderoga in New York.

EVENT

By chaining logs to a cart pulled by a team of horses, Vermont loggers "skidded" their logs out of the forest.

original states, now that America was free from English rule, Vermont wanted to be part of the new country. On March 4, 1791, Vermont became the 14th state in the U.S. At that time, there were approximately 85,000 people living in Vermont.

After Vermont became a state, its population grew quickly. By 1810, the population was 217,895. Many of Vermont's settlers made their living growing wheat, oats, and barley. Some cut down the state's towering trees to make potash, a chemical that was used to dye wool. Others brought livestock to the land. By the mid-1830s, about two million sheep were grazing in the state. But as the U.S. expanded in the late 1800s, many of those sheep were moved west. They were replaced by dairy cows.

The dairy industry grew rapidly in Vermont. Although the number of people in the state grew in the early 1900s, the number of cows grew faster. Some reports say that by 1930, there were 421,000 cows in Vermont but only 359,000 people.

Vermont dairy workers moved from milking by hand to using milking machines in the early 1900s.

YEAR

1777 Vermont settlers declare their territory an independent republic and write their own constitution.

EVENT

Hills and Valleys

Vermont is one of six states in the northeastern U.S. that make up a region known as New England. It is the only state in the region that does not touch the Atlantic Ocean. Vermont sits between New York to the west and New Hampshire to the east. Canada is on its northern border, while Massachusetts is to the south.

Vermont is the sixth-smallest state in the U.S. From top to bottom, it measures 157 miles (253 km). But it has many different landscapes. That's because thousands of years ago, sheets of ice called glaciers covered the state. When the glaciers moved, they carved out tall mountains and deep valleys.

The Green Mountains rise up in the middle of Vermont and stretch from north to south. The Taconic Range occupies the southwestern corner of the state. On both the eastern and western edges of Vermont, the land is much flatter. In the east, the flatlands are called the Vermont Piedmont because "piedmont" means "at the foot of the mountains." The Vermont and Champlain valleys are west of the Green Mountains.

Vermont's brilliant fall foliage can be seen in its hilly northern regions (opposite) as well as in its flat eastern and western lands (above).

Glaciers also created hundreds of deep, clear lakes and fast-moving rivers in Vermont. There are more than 400 lakes in the state. The largest is Lake Champlain, which forms part of the state's border with New York. Since Samuel de Champlain first saw Lake Champlain in 1609, there have been rumors about a sea monster living in its depths. Champlain wrote about an eight-foot-long (2.4 m) creature that snatched birds out of the air. That monster, whether real or imagined, has become known in the area as "Champ."

The rolling hills and flatlands of Vermont are good for farming. Apple trees bloom in the northwest. Oats and hay are grown in other areas. They help feed the approximately 150,000 dairy cows that live in Vermont today.

While hay is primarily grown in the fields of eastern Vermont (above), Lake Champlain (opposite) dominates the western border of the state between the Green Mountains and New York's Adirondacks.

At Rock of Ages granite quarry near Barre, workers are lowered 600 feet (183 m) to reach the bottom.

But in much of the state, farming is difficult. That is because, in many areas, hard stones such as granite, marble, and slate lie just below the surface. Stone quarries are found throughout these regions. Quarries are deep holes in the earth where the rock is dug out and carried away. The largest underground marble quarry in the world is in the southwestern town of Danby. The rocks taken out of Vermont's quarries are used to build impressive buildings and monuments, including Vermont's state capitol in Montpelier.

Vermont's varied landscape is best suited for hardy plants and trees. More than a dozen species of fern grow in the state. Maples, pines, and hardwoods such as ash and hickory also thrive. The forests are home to many animals, including bears, moose, and white-tailed deer. Smaller animals, such as beavers and woodchucks, are also found in Vermont.

Vermont is known for its cold winters and mild summers. Temperatures often dip below freezing in the winter. The average temperature is between 25 and 30 °F (-4 to -1 °C). Up to 80 inches (203 cm) of snow falls between November and March. The snow may be as deep as 300 inches (762 cm) in the mountains. In the summer, temperatures usually stay between 68 and 95 °F (20 to 35 °C). Although there are a few hot and humid days, it is generally so mild that many cars and buildings do not need to have air conditioning.

A white-tailed deer's reddish-brown coat changes to a gray-brown color during the fall and winter.

YEAR

1816 A June blizzard drops a foot (30 cm) of snow in Vermont, and freezing conditions continue through September.

EVENT

Living off the Land

BETWEEN THE FRIGID WINTER WEATHER, THE DANGEROUS MOUNTAINS, AND THE ROCKY SOIL, LIFE IN VERMONT CAN BE DIFFICULT. MOST NATIVES APPRECIATE THE CHALLENGE. LIKE THE EARLY EUROPEANS WHO SETTLED THE STATE, THEY CONSIDER THEMSELVES TO BE CAPABLE AND TOUGH.

Many Vermont families have lived in the area for several generations. Some have stayed since settling there in the 1600s and 1700s. Many people make a living off the land. They plant maple trees to make maple syrup or grow apple trees. They log timber to make paper and furniture or mine for granite, marble, and slate.

Since the late 1800s, Vermonters have also raised dairy cows. Although the number of dairy farms in Vermont is decreasing, milk and cheese are still important products, and so is ice cream. In 1978, Ben Cohen and Jerry Greenfield opened the first Ben & Jerry's Homemade Ice Cream Scoop Shop in downtown Burlington. Since then, their funny-sounding flavors, such as Chunky Monkey and Cherry Garcia, have become favorites all over the world.

Even in the cold and snow, when much firewood needs to be burned (opposite), Vermonters still enjoy Ben & Jerry's ice cream (above).

YEAR

1846   The first postage stamp used in the U.S. is printed in Brattleboro.

EVENT

Chester A. Arthur (top) was born near Lake Champlain, while Calvin Coolidge (bottom) grew up in the central part of the state.

Most people think of milk, ice cream, and cheese when they think of Vermont. But the state makes more electronic equipment than food. It also produces computer parts and metal products, including guns.

Two U.S. presidents were also "products" of Vermont. Chester A. Arthur grew up in Fairfield. He became the country's 21st president in 1881, when James A. Garfield was assassinated. In 1923, Calvin Coolidge, who was born in Plymouth, became president when Warren G. Harding died. He was elected to a full four-year term in 1924.

Vermont's rugged landscape and natural beauty have also made it a great place for creative people to produce their work. Poet Robert Frost moved to Vermont as an adult to better write about the state's beauty. Famous artist Norman Rockwell often used his neighbors in the town of Arlington as models for his illustrations. Skier Billy Kidd was born and raised in

Norman Rockwell worked in a pine-paneled studio while living in an Arlington farmhouse from 1943 to 1953.

YEAR

1911   Vermont establishes a Bureau of Publicity to attract tourists to the state.

EVENT

- 20 -

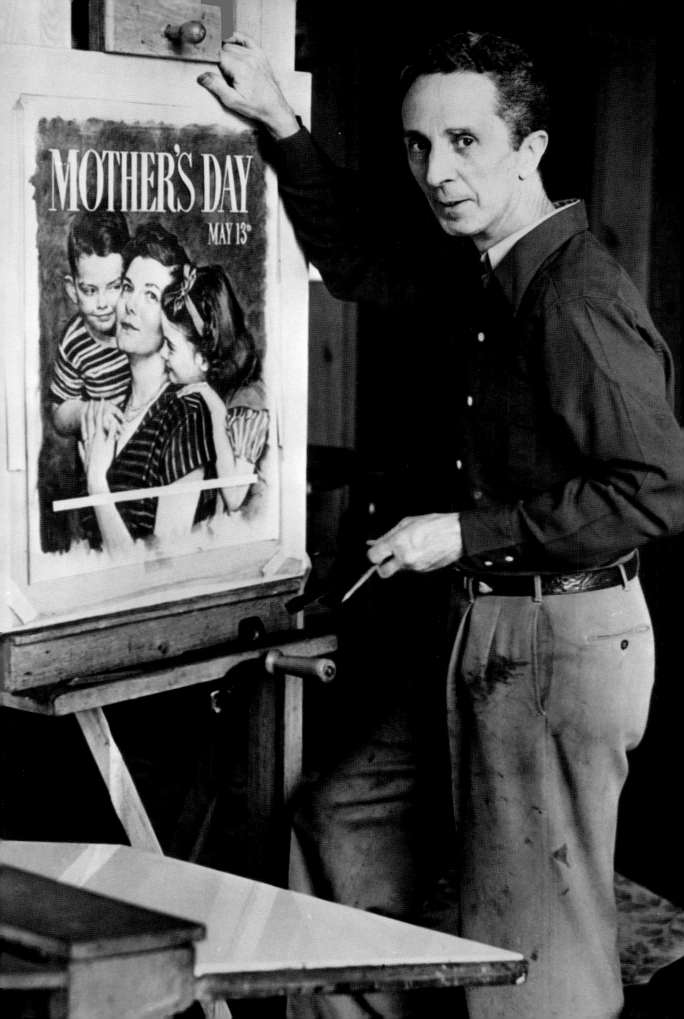

Stowe, where he spent most of his time on the ski hills. In 1964, he became the first American man to earn an Olympic medal in alpine skiing.

Montpelier, which means "bare hill," was named after the French city of the same name in 1781.

Although Vermont's mountains and forests provide plenty of opportunities for recreation, they have also limited the state's population growth. Almost 622,000 people live in Vermont. Only one state, Wyoming, has fewer people. Some population experts predict that by 2025 Vermont could be the least-populated state.

Part of the reason for this is that there are very few growing cities in Vermont. About 70 percent of the state's population lives outside of cities or in towns with fewer than 2,500 people. The biggest city in Vermont is Burlington, where almost 40,000 people live. The capital city of Montpelier is home to approximately 8,000 people. That makes it the smallest state capital in the country.

After winning the silver medal in slalom at the 1964 Olympics, Billy Kidd failed to place at the 1968 Games.

YEAR

1923 Vermont native Calvin Coolidge becomes the 30th U.S. president.

EVENT

Vermont lumber

Montpelier, 1927

The majority of Vermont's population is white. American Indians, whose villages once surrounded Lake Champlain and the Missisquoi River, now make up less than one percent of the population. Asian Americans and African Americans account for only about one percent each.

The influence of French explorers can still be seen and heard in Vermont. More than 17,000 residents speak French in their homes. Vermont borders the Canadian province of Quebec, where many people speak French. When French Canadians immigrated to Vermont to find jobs in the logging industry, they brought their language with them.

After the Winooski River flooded in 1927, devastating Vermont towns such as the capital of Montpelier (opposite), the state needed help from its lumber industry (above) to rebuild.

The Winooski River floods as heavy rains swamp the state, killing at least 60 people.

Only in Vermont

Visiting Vermont can sometimes seem like a trip into the past. The state has worked hard to preserve its history and what natives call "the simple life." That is why it has maintained more than 100 covered bridges in the state for almost 200 years.

Vermont's covered bridges were first built in the early 1800s. The walls and roofs protected travelers and their horses as they crossed icy rivers during the cold, windy winters. Many of the original bridges are still standing. The oldest is the Pulp Mill Bridge. Built in 1820, it still crosses Otter Creek, near Middlebury. The Cornish-Windsor Bridge crosses the Connecticut River. At 449 feet (137 m), it is the second-longest wooden covered bridge in the country.

Another common sight in Vermont is maple trees. The tradition of collecting syrup from sugar maples began with the American Indians. They taught the settlers how to do it, and modern Vermonters continue the tradition today. Each spring, people drill holes in the trees and attach either spigots (which are like faucets) or plastic tubes. They collect the sweet sap that flows from the holes in big buckets. The sap is boiled down to make syrup. It takes 35 to 40 gallons (130–150 l) of sap to make 1 gallon (3.8 l) of maple syrup.

Sugar shacks are usually small, wooden buildings where sap is taken to be boiled into maple sugar.

The Cornish-Windsor Bridge connects the towns of Cornish, New Hampshire, and Windsor, Vermont.

YEAR

1945 President Harry Truman names Vermont senator Warren Austin as the first U.S. ambassador to the United Nations.

EVENT

Vermont produces more maple syrup than any other state. It then sells the syrup throughout the country. Many Vermonters dribble hot maple syrup over a cup of clean, freshly fallen snow. Some even eat dill pickles with the sweet treat. It's all part of Vermont tradition!

Another Vermont tradition is hiking in the mountains. The oldest hiking trail in the country follows the Green Mountains for 270 miles (435 km) from north to south. Fall is a favorite time to explore the state's forests. The leaves of hardwoods such as ash and cottonwoods usually turn such pretty colors that people come from far away to see them. Vermonters call those visitors "leaf peepers."

Vermont's mountains make the state a great place to ski as well. The country's first tow rope to pull skiers up a mountain was installed in Vermont in 1934. In 1940, the first chairlift in the country was built on Mount Mansfield, near Stowe. Today, dozens of ski resorts are nestled in Vermont's mountains.

A casual hiker can rest and enjoy the view of northeastern Vermont (above), but a downhill skier is always on the move (opposite).

YEAR

1985   Madeleine M. Kunin becomes the state's first female governor.

EVENT

- 28 -

QUICK FACTS

Population: 621,254

Largest city: Burlington (pop. 38,531)

Capital: Montpelier

Entered the union: March 4, 1791

Nickname: Green Mountain State

State flower: red clover

State bird: hermit thrush

Size: 9,614 sq mi (24,900 sq km)—45th-biggest in U.S.

Major industries: manufacturing, tourism, farming, mining, logging

Skiing may be the most popular sport in Vermont. No professional sports teams are located in the state, but there is a semi-professional football team. The Vermont Ice Storm have been playing in the Empire Football League since 2001. In 2007, the Ice Storm had an undefeated 15–0 season.

Ski hills and bright fall colors have made Vermont a favorite tourist destination. But at one time, the state's many visitors threatened its lakes, rivers, and beautiful landscape. In 1970, Vermont passed the Environmental Control Law, making it the first state to legally protect its environment. The law limits development projects and makes sure no harm is done to the state's natural resources.

Vermont's commitment to its natural resources will preserve the state's assets for generations. Vermonters are proud of their rural lifestyle. They work hard to keep their state pristine. Its rugged mountains, crystal clear lakes, and rolling green hills make Vermont a beautiful place to live or to visit.

YEAR

2004   Former Vermont governor Howard Dean runs for the Democratic nomination for president.

EVENT

BIBLIOGRAPHY

Duffy, John. *Vermont: An Illustrated History.* Northridge, Calif.: Windsor Publications, 1985.

Eagleson, Janet, and Rosemary Hasner. *The Maple Syrup Book.* Erin, Ontario: Boston Mills Press, 2006.

McDevitt, Neale, ed. *New England.* New York: DK Publishing, 2007.

Mitchell, Don. *Compass American Guides: Vermont.* New York: Compass American Guides/Fodor's Travel Publications, 2001.

Vermont Division for Historic Preservation. "Homepage." Vermont Division for Historic Preservation. http://www .historicvermont.org.

INDEX